Seasons

Seasons

Poems

Nol Alembong

SPEARS BOOKS
Denver, Colorado

Spears Books
An Imprint of Spears Media Press LLC
7830 W. Alameda Ave, Suite 103-247
Denver, CO 80226
United States of America

First Published in the United States of America in 2025 by Spears Books
www.spearsbooks.org
info@spearsmedia.com
Information on this title: www.spearsbooks.org/seasons

© 2025 Nol Alembong
All rights reserved.

No part of this publication may be reproduced, distributed, or transmitted in any form or by any means, including photocopying, recording, or other electronic or mechanical methods, without the prior written permission of the publisher, except in the case of brief quotations embodied in critical reviews and certain other noncommercial uses permitted by copyright law. For permission requests, write to the publisher, addressed "Attention: Permissions Coordinator," at the above address.

ISBN: 9781957296555 (Paperback)
ISBN: 9781957296562 (eBook)

Spears Media Press has no responsibility for the persistence or accuracy of urls for external or third-party internet websites referred to in this publication, and does not guarantee that any content on such websites is, or will remain, accurate or appropriate.

Designed and typeset by Spears Media Press LLC
Cover Design: Doh Kambem

Distributed globally by African Books Collective (ABC)
www.africanbookscollective.com

Contents

Foreword ✦ ix

SEASON 1: CREEDS   XV

Spiritus Mundi Credo ✦ 1
Hominum Credo ✦ 2
Animal Credo ✦ 3
Plebi Credo ✦ 5
Inanimata Mundi Credo ✦ 6

SEASON 2: RETROSPECTION   7

I Sing of Government High School Mamfe ✦ 8
I Sing of Professor Paul Mbangwana ✦ 10
Marriage Vows ✦ 12
Umbrellas for Grey Brains ✦ 14
When Mr Leopard Finally Passed On ✦ 18

SEASON 3: DESIRE   19

Amazing Green ✦ 20
Carrefour de beaucoup de bars ✦ 21
For Better and for Worse ✦ 23
One Night in Heaven ✦ 24
Take Me to Jerusalem ✦ 26

SEASON 4: ECSTASY 27

Eve at Birth • 28
Lebong at Birth • 29
ML, the Fairest Flower from Cupid • 30
Rose • 32
The Last Virgin • 33

SEASON 5: FULFILMENT 35

First Rains • 36
Half Widows • 37
Joy-stick • 38
Love Letter • 39
Taboo Love • 41

SEASON 6: RAVENING 43

Dating • 44
March 8 • 46
Men of God • 47
Symptoms • 50
Valentine Gift • 51

SEASON 7: ENTREATIES 53

Before You Sleep • 54
GHS Mamfe • 56
Money or Grammar? • 58
One Eye • 59
Wartime Ladies • 60

SEASON 8: RIPPLES   63

    Massa Talk-Talk Dem ✦ 64
    Night Waka ✦ 66
    Njakri Tok ✦ 67
    Ripples in the Pond ✦ 68
    WhatsApp Chats ✦ 69

SEASON 9: REVOLT   71

    Dis War Sef ✦ 72
    He Ascended into Hell ✦ 74
    Pikin Soldier Dem ✦ 76
    Shithole ✦ 78
    Wood Power ✦ 80

SEASON 10: STARLIGHT   83

    Andong's Tongue ✦ 84
    Tale Time ✦ 87
    The Day You Shall Finally Leave ✦ 96
    The Resurrection ✦ 97
    You Too May Carry A Cross ✦ 99

About the Author ✦ 105

Foreword

The scholastics argue that *tempora mutantur, nos et mutamur illis* - a Latin aphorism which could be loosely translated as times change and any rational being must change with them. It goes without saying that a man who refuses to make adjustments dictated by the passage of time is not different from the stubborn and brainless tree in the story that wanted to wrestle with the passing wind, instead of bending its head to let it pass, and was broken down by the wind. This is the situation in which contemporary African writers find themselves and the sagacious ones are adjusting their discursive and aesthetic orientations dictated on them by the different events and situations in Africa and the global world at large. Most of these writers address climate change, environmentalism, identity crises, globalisation, terrorism, human rights, war, and the political hypocrisy of the international system. Those who are current in national and international politics will subscribe to the view that the above issue is trendy in the global community. Postcolonial writers explore and articulate these problematic issues in their works with the solemn intention of making their voices heard amidst other voices. Nol Alembong's collection of poems entitled *Seasons* falls within the works that capture the spirit of the time, both at the aesthetic and discursive levels.

In this regard, Chinua Achebe, in *There Was a Country: A Personal History of Biafra,* postulates that "the role of the writer is not a rigid position and depends to some extent on the state of health of his or her society. In other words, if a society is ill, the writer has the responsibility to point it out. If the society is healthier, the writer's job is different" (57). Nol Alembong, in *Seasons,* presents a postcolonial/contemporary political society infested by a plethora of maladies and malaises. He is among the Cameroonian/African poets adjusting their thematic orientations to the changing contexts of their time. He has a keen attention on the burning issues of his time, and these issues find expression or inroads in his poetic idioms. His present collection of poems is testimony to this fact that Alembong's poetry handles issues that have imposed themselves in contemporary times and, as a poet-philosopher, he approaches them from a philosophico-aesthetic dimension in the hope that they may change as the seasons change for the betterment off all and sundry—a critical posture which is in tandem with the Marxist hermeneutics that philosophers have described the world around them and it is now time to change it. The English novelist and essayist, George Orwell, in his 1946 essay "Why I Write," further corroborates the above idea when he contends that his purpose of writing is to alter the way people look at the world and make them change their mindset.

This present collection, *Seasons*, consists of fifty poems divided into different seasons—from season one to season ten. Since writers are social beings who live in society among their kind and are affected by socio-political, economic, and cultural happenings in their various societies, the poems in this collection are semiotic representations of thematic and discursive issues deeply rooted in the postcolonial and contemporary society. What is critically peculiar about this collection is Alembong's insightful use of animal and nature imagery to discuss contemporary leitmotifs. His strong attachment to nature and environmental aesthetics makes him stand out as a 21st-century African Romantic poet. Also, the *prima facie* structures and shapes of the poems in this collection give the reader a clue to the meaning and significations of each poem in the collection.

One discourse that finds sufficient space in this present collection is the idea of African spirituality, metaphysics, and identity. This thematic discourse is found in "Spiritus Mundi Credo," where the poet handles issues of African spirituality, communitarianism, metaphysics, and the relationship between the living and the dead in African mythology. The "spirits" in this poem are the ancestors who have gone to the world beyond and united in the "world of spiritual realms." While in this world they are aware of their role—"to look after those left behind" (5). African spirituality in this poem is in corroboration of John S. Mbiti's affirmations in *African Religions and Philosophy* that "The spiritual world of African peoples is very populated with spiritual beings, spirits of the living-dead" and "Their insight of spiritual realities, whether absolute or apparent, is extremely sharp" (74). This poem instills fresh confidence in the living that they are not alone, as the ancestors watch over them in guidance. By so doing, the poet is also exhorting the living to have the spirit of Ubuntu in their daily activities because if their ancestors can be so united among themselves in the land of the dead, it is also a clarion call for the living to copy their behaviour and live in the spirit of Ubuntu. Notwithstanding, in "Plebi Credo", the poet depicts the idea of identity and African socialism. This use of the collective pronoun "We" demonstrates the unity of these people with a "unique essence" who believe that "one flower makes no garland." In other words, the poet drives home the ideology that "united we stand and divided we fall." A similar idea also runs through the poem "Inanimata Mundi Credo," where the poet pontificates that everything has importance and no one should despise anything.

Another discursive issue that permeates the entire collection is the poet's ecological or environmental consciousness. The poet's ideological orientation is tailored towards the preservation of the postcolonial/contemporary natural environment in the present context of the Anthropocene. In this context, Susan Board, in *Ecological Relations: Towards an Inclusive Politics of the Earth*, notes that the ecological environment cannot be excluded in the practice of International Relations since ecological foundations are the bedrocks of human relations. Thus, "an ecological paradigm" she argues "would compel us to recognise our biological and social embeddedness and interdependence with particular temporal and ecosystemic contexts" and "It would require a rejection of traditional epistemological principles that legitimise the 'exploitation and liquidation of nonhuman nature', based upon a homocentric ethics and teleology" (38). Board's ecological perspective is also distilled in most of the poems in this collection, where Alembong conscientizes the postcolonial and contemporary world of the importance of nature and why ecological/environmental protection is a categorical imperative. The poet presents himself as an African romantic/nature poet whose ideological tapestry is to protect the natural environment at all cost against eco-marauders! In "Hominum Credo," Alembong glorifies nature in the colour "green." According to him, green is "the giver of life," because "in the beginning was green and green shall always be." The poet's glorification and somewhat deification of nature indicate that environmental protection and conservation are a clarion call for all and sundry to indulge in. This leitmotif of eco-protection is also radiated in "Animal Credo", "Amazing Green", "ML, the Fairest Flower from Cupid," "Rose," "First Rain," "Love Letter," etc.

Alembong, in this present collection, is of the pacifist ideology that war should not be encouraged in the postcolonial society because it benefits neither of the parties involved in the conflicts. He believes that every problem can be solved in a peaceful and pacified manner without necessarily going to war, because war has negative consequences for both sides. It lays the foundation for violence, hardship, misery, hatred, underdevelopment, and a life of trauma. Achille Mbembe in *On the Postcolony* argues that one of the visible signposts of postcolonial Africa is the internecine violence in most post-colonial African states. He notes, "The violence of war and control of the means of coercion weigh decisively today in the organisation of postcolonial societies" (88). In "Dis War Sef" and "Pikin Soldier Dem," two poems written in refined Pidgin English, the poet discusses the horrors of war and expresses his disgust in this warlike situation. According to the poet, as exemplified in "Dis War Sef," war has terrible consequences and casualties on both sides of the divide because during a situation of war, "Lion people dem lie everywhere / Hyena people dem lie everywhere / Wolf people dem lie everywhere / Who go carry who? / Who go bury who?" These rhetorical questions show the confusion and disorder that reign in a situation of war. The poet-persona, at the end of the poem, recommends that to solve the problem of "palapala field," all and sundry must sit under the "mboma tree" and dialogue for peace to reign in the "palapala field." The negative consequences and connotations of war are also vividly articulated and enunciated in "Pikin Soldier Dem," where the poet vehemently vituperates the phenomenon of child combatants or soldiers in postcolonial societies.

In addition, political hypocrisy, falsehood, and the crisis of leadership are also found in Alembong's recent collection. These vices have enshrined themselves as political culture in most postcolonial societies. In the opening lines of his book *Political Hypocrisy*, David Runciman comments, "There is a lot of hypocrisy at work in contemporary politics" (1). In "Massa Talk-Talk Dem," the poet lampoons the culture of political hypocrisy in the global society. The speaker in the poem argues that in the past, people were honest and their pronouncements could be taken for what they were—which is not the case in modern times especially among politicians. Apart from this strong culture of hypocrisy in modern politics, the poet affirms that a badly governed country will only lay the foundation for future political and social cataclysm. In "Wood Power," the poet uses the image of the forest to discuss irresponsible governance, leadership, and tyranny in postcolonial societies, where "the wood" in the poem is an imagistic representation of the postcolonial nation-state. In the first part of the poem, the poet-persona notes that "the wood" was "lively, dense, and deep" with animals living in harmony with one another before the "tortoise crawled in with his big sense" and began constraining the other animals to behave like him—an attitude that caused a revolt in the wood. This poem has multilayers of meaning and could also be interpreted as a historical allusion to colonialism, which eventually laid the groundwork for imperialism and neo-colonialism in most postcolonial states. Similarly, in "The Day You Shall Finally Leave," the poet handles issues of political change, expectation, and nation-building—a theme also found in "Before You Sleep."

Finally, Nol Alembong is also interested in social relations and role-modelling. He criticises irresponsible and social hypocrites and fair-weather friends whose visions of creating relationships are for exploitative propensities. He believes that social relationships should carry the Ubuntu spirit of communalism and togetherness. This is because the African society, in its essence, is communitarian in nature and not individualistic. In "Dating," for instance, the poet-persona uses a sarcastic undertone to criticise relationships that are motivated by materialism and cupidity. He satirises the different groups of people indulging in this dating phenomenon. He criticises scammers, lawyers, teachers, politicians, classmates, policemen, cashiers, footballers, managers, and tradi-practitioners who indulge in this business of dating and using tricks when they are sought for. The poem, therefore, is a caustic satire on hypocrisy, which is demonstrated in most social relationships in contemporary society. The phenomenon of an exploitative relationship is also treated in "March 8," "Symptoms," and "Valentine Gift," where the poems also remonstrate against those who get into social relationships with an exigent and exploitative mindset.

In conclusion, Nol Alembong's *Seasons* is a collection that interrogates the contemporary world on the vices which have almost expressed themselves as normality. The greatness of the poems in this collection is anchored on the unvarnished fact that the poems have multiple layers of meaning, coupled with the fact that they are endowed with aesthetic affinity because Alembong is not only interested in the philosophy that lies underneath the poems, but also in their artistic propriety. This is to acquiesce to Mikhail Bakhtin's view that form and content in discourse are one and indivisible.

Eric Nsuh Zuhmboshi, PhD
Associate Professor
Department of African Literature and Civilisations
The University of Yaounde I, Cameroon

SEASON 1

CREEDS

Spiritus Mundi Credo

We are spirits,
We believe in our world,
The world of spiritual realms,
In which we live like in any realm in creation,
In houses and in compounds of our own making
With our spouses, children, kin relations and friends,
In union with the forces that command universal existence.

We are spirits,
We believe in our essence:
An essence unknown to mortals,
An essence that guides the individual spirit,
An essence that binds us as a community of spirits,
An essence that compels us to be each other's keeper,
An essence that compels us to look after those left behind.

Hominum Credo

We believe in green, the giver of life,
Located on earth and at the centre of spectrum,
Guarantor of growth, renewal, vitality, balance and life,
For in the beginning was green and green shall always be.

We believe in the freshness green brings,
Green gives us food, water, shelter, and health,
Green gives us balm, vigour, drive, elegance and peace,
For in the beginning was green and green shall always be.

We believe in the harmony green brings,
In green we find a blend of nature and life itself,
In green we find a blend of love, joy, hope and eternal life,
For in the beginning was green and green shall always be.

In green we shall sing.
In green we shall dance.
In green we shall play
In green we shall feast

In green we shall bath
In green we shall sleep
In green we shall love
In green we shall rise

In green we shall dream
In green we shall find
In green we shall grow
Till the end of the earth.

Animal Credo

We believe in Silvanus, our Father Almighty,
The Almighty Owner of the woods we live in.
Protector of the forest and its entire boundaries,
Once laid in waste like land ripped by tornadoes;
Protector of all cultivated and uncultivated lands,
Once bare like fields ravaged by angry hurricanes;
Protector of all trees, in bud and growing strong alike
Once bowing under the weight of ever-raging tempests;
Protector of all animals, whose homes are in his woods,
Once the hunting ground of invisible blood-thirsty spirits.

We believe in his ever-open and watchful eyes
He watches over the fields and its boundaries,
He watches over every single ape in its logging,
He watches over every single badger in its hole,
He watches over every single beaver in its lodge,
He watches over every single bird in its nest,
He watches over every single cow in its stable.
He watches over every single goat in its locker,
He watches over every single rabbit in its burrow,
He watches over every single squirrel in its drey.

We believe in him and in his forgiveness of sins.
His forgiveness of the lion that preys on warthogs;
His forgiveness of the tiger that preys on young rhinos;
His forgiveness of the leopard that preys on antelopes;
His forgiveness of the hyena that preys on hares;
His forgiveness of the harpy eagle that preys on monkeys;
His forgiveness of the hawk that preys on chickens;
His forgiveness of the python that preys on deer;
His forgiveness of the viper that preys on lizards;
And in his forgiveness of the penguin that preys on shrimps.

We believe in Silvanus,
The Owner and Protector of the woods;
We believe in him till the end of time
When we would have crossed the Lethe,
When no one will be judged for what he did
Or for what he failed to do in the woods.

Plebi Credo

We believe in our unique existence,
In our one and indivisible Regnum Plantae,
In the unity of cryptogams and phanerogams,
In the sisterhood of flowering and nonflowering plants,
In the binding sisterhood of seed-bearing and seedless plants,
And in the unwavering brotherhood of aquatic and terrestrial plants.

We believe in our power of communication
In our power of communication through chemical signals
Through our ability to sense and respond to environmental cues
Through the ability of our root system to gather and share ground secrets
Through the production of sensitive sounds alerting others of changing times
And through making known our fundamental role of shaping the earth's ecosystem.

We truly believe that one flower
Makes no garland; never, never.
We believe that no one among us
Can make Regnum Plantae alone.
We believe that we grow straight
When we by each other in the fold.

We believe in the sisterhood of plants,
We believe in the brotherhood of plants:
We always talk and listen to each other,
We pollinate ourselves and each other,
We sow courtesy and reap friendship
We sow kindness and reap lasting love.

Inanimata Mundi Credo

We, said to be non-living things,
Believe in ourselves for what we are.
We believe in the unity and power of our world,
For we live not only for ourselves but for humanity.

Who says I, Air, have no life?
I give people life when they are born.
I withdraw their breath and so they die.
Hence, like Water, I am the giver and taker of life.

Who says I, Water, have no life?
I give people life when they drink me.
They do not have life when I am not there.
Hence, like Air, I am the giver and taker of life.

Who says we, Rocks, have no life?
We give the universe the environment it needs.
We have the ability to influence shape and habitats.
Hence, like Air and Water, we make the universe what it is.

Who says I, Gold, have no life?
I make nations laugh when they have me.
I make nations cry when they do not have me.
Hence I am the maker and mover of the entire world.

Who says we have no eternal presence?
Who says we do not have a sense of the past?
Who says we do not have a sense of the future?
We believe in our histories and in our sense of purpose.

SEASON 2

RETROSPECTION

I Sing of Government High School Mamfe

Decades have rolled by, slowly rolled by,
Like a tired, idle moon crossing a town asleep.
Yes, five decades and four years have rolled by
When we arrived that hot river town of Mamfe
Traversing dense forests and sparse savannahs.

First arrivals always drink the purest flow
So it is that early birds, emerging from warm nests,
Catch the fattest worms released by the night soil.
And so, we arrived that hot river town of Mamfe
To drink from the fountain flowing from Manyu.

When we arrived, we found an iroko on which to climb,
Yes, we found an iroko, Mr. Sampson Atem Ako-Arrey,
For where there is a big and strong tree in a dense forest
Small ones climb on its back to reach the far away sun
And learn to sing and talk like the big and strong tree itself.

Around that strong iroko were other trees, lending support,
Keeping the air fresh, protecting us from uncertain winds,
Storing fresh water for us during times of severe drought
Sucking up extra water when it rained a lot, like never before,
Producing cones and pollen to help us reproduce and stand strong.

We settled on our books, like bees settling on flowers for nectar,
Some unsure of where birds ever retire to roost when the sun sleeps,
Some not knowing how any woman's kitchen around ever looked like,
Some not knowing how long nights were or why owls slept with open eyes,
Some not knowing for true that rain does not fall on one roof alone.

A good doe knows where her calves will sleep, prowling wolves in her

mind.
A good hen knows where her chicks will sleep, predatory birds in her mind.
The calves and chicks who showed up in that hot town by the graceful Manyu
With no does and bucks, with no hens and cocks, that accompanied them,
Found a good doe, found a good hen, in the person of one Madam Orock.

Yes, a home without a woman is like a barn without a shepherd.
Who will provide hay to hungry sheep when the going is rough?
Who will provide hay diets to sheep in need of something else?
Who will take the sheep to the fields when they need fresh greens?
Who will tell the story of the barn by the fireside when the sun has gone to sleep?

When we settled on our mission, we were like the chameleon,
For the chameleon changes colours to match the earth,
The earth does not change colours to match the chameleon.
In five years, we were like birds that fly from the ground
Birds that fly from the ground onto a baobab tree to reach the sun.

And today I sing of Government High School Mamfe
Lying by the banks of the graceful and lovely Manyu
In that sunny town that forever produces roses and daisies
Whose delicate fragrance makes Cameroon smell nice to all
Whose fine colours, like the rainbow, brighten the Globe.

I Sing of Professor Paul Mbangwana

Decades have rolled by
Like a lazy moon crossing a town
When we arrived the mountain spring
Wading through freezing morning dew.

First arrivals always drink the purest flow
So it is that early birds catch the fattest worms.
We arrived later but the water was still as pure as dew
For the spring was never made to be stirred by early ducks.

When we arrived
We found an iroko on which to climb
For where there is a big and strong tree
Small ones climb on its back to reach the sun
And learn to sing and talk like the tree itself.

When we settled
We found a dog that does not put a juicy bone in its puppies' mouths
For he who puts a juicy bone in a child's mouth
Wants to prevent him from barking
Even when in the house of death.

When we settled
We found a bird that flies from the ground onto a baobab tree
But knows that it is still on the ground
For the chameleon changes colours to match the earth
The earth doesn't change colours to match the chameleon.

When we settled
We found a cat that does not eat its own kittens
For when a cat wants to eat its own kittens
It accuses them of smelling like rats.

When we settled
We found a turtle that lays thousands of eggs without anyone knowing
Unlike hens that inform the whole country when they lay just an egg.

When we settled
We found an elephant that does not limp when walking on thorns
Or that is not overpowered by its own tusks.

When we settled
We found a palm tree that encourages birds to nest in it
And does not cry over shattered leaves.

When we settled
We found a rooster that crows for the whole world
When others crow for their immediate neighbourhoods.

Prof,
Should I compare you to a hunter?
The hunter who is tracking an elephant
Does not stop to throw stones at birds
But you always stopped to throw stones at birds
Knowing that birds in flight may have eggs in their stomachs.

Or
Should I compare you to the eagle?
Though the sky belongs to the eagle
It can't fly when it's raining
But your wings were made to brave the storm
The way owls brave the darkest night.

Marriage Vows

Once upon a time
Away from a big troop of mountain monkeys
Was found a lovely bevy of female monkeys
In which lived Annie a cute calm life of grace.

Hairy like an Afghan hound, greasy plump face,
Eyes as bright as comets around the sun at noon,
Plump chest and body like that of a fat porpoise,
Annie was the fairest of the fair in the entire bevy.

A goat came by, eyed her and stared into space.
He gazed at her and swallowed his own spittle
His hidden love for her appearing like misty rain
Coming softly but flooding the river in his heart.

Come on, ride on, his heart seemed to tell him,
He who truly loves a vase loves also what is inside,
No shortcuts exist to the top of the tallest palm tree.
This urge from his heart could be read on his face.

His heart was like wood already touched by fire, for
Wood already touched by fire is not hard to set alight.
So he stepped forward and sang sweet songs of love
That made Annie's ears stand like those of a rabbit.

The day after, like a breeze that sweeps across shores,
The deed was sealed with a vow witnessed by sparrows:
I, Goat, take you, Annie, to be my wife for better, for worse.
I, Annie, take you, Goat, to be my husband for better, for better.

That day, Annie's face shone like a mirror in the midday sun
Her eyes burning like fire, her lips red like a bleeding wound.

She stood like a full moon set aside in an orbit of its own; ah!
The surface of water is beautiful, but it is not good to sleep on.

These several seasons of the union, Annie is in her tree home
Like bats roosting in trees or in dark caves for fear of the sun.
These several seasons of the union, the goat is on the ground
Like moles in sealed burrows beneath hot clay in the savannah.

On judgement day both will explain the meaning of their vows.
Every deed will be brought into judgement, good and evil alike,
And each person will simply receive what is due for him or her
And it will come to pass that every secret will be brought to light.

Umbrellas for Grey Brains

You
and me.
have lived together,
played on the same fields,
in our infant nakedness, attended
the same schools as we moved from
town to town and to the capital city to cap
it
all.
So
it's
you
and
me
all
the
time
being together.

You
and me
toiled in the capital
reading volumes of books to
earn good scores and climb further
and reach the harvest sun for the fruits
of future years. We got there and felt the
joy,
saw
the
way
to
fine
life,
the
way
to
mine for gold.

You
and me
got to the vast farm
sparkling with ackees, apples,
apricots, bananas, blueberries, cherries,
figs, grapes, guavas, kiwis, lemon and oranges.
Lads with grey brains with God fathers as umbrellas
got
all
and
we
with
fine
jell
got
not
even
unripe ones

Grey
brains need
umbrellas in the
wet and dry seasons, for fear of
the icy hands of rain and for fear of the
hot embrace of the jubilant sun. But rain beats the
leopard's skin but it does not wash out the spots and
the
sun
is
for
all
to
see
and
feel;
even
blind bats, too.

When Mr Leopard Finally Passed On

When Mr Leopard commandeered their lives
He prowled alone like a rhinoceros
Unable to see the trails through the forest
Used by the multitude of forest dwellers
In their endless search for food.

The man dies who prowls and screams alone
Like a fierce hyena that ends up receiving the spear.
The man dies who considers himself a buffalo
Like the frog that got killed, considering itself an elephant.
So did Mr Leopard pass on like the fierce hyena and the proud frog.

When he finally passed on, the land glowed with rainbow colours.
Grey slowly gave way to the moon, and the moon to the rising sun.
The animals emerged from their holes, like slugs leaving the earth.
Moles came with tubers, toads with water and monkeys with wood
And when the feast was ready everyone ate and said YES.

SEASON 3

DESIRE

Amazing Green

   Amazing green of all my dreams
   I trod the wide Amazon to seek thee
   I trod Tuckerman Ravine to seek thee
   I followed the fast Nile to seek thee
   I scaled the great Everest to seek thee.

   And when the lizard nodded at me,
   When the cock's crow rent the air,
   When the praying mantis prayed,
   And the rainbow appeared above
   I found thee, like a leper, a balm.

   I was truly blind, but now I see.
   I was truly deaf, but now I hear.
   I was truly dumb, but now I talk.
   Since I found thee, yes found thee,
   Amazing green of all my dreams.

   Take hold of me, take hold of me,
   Amazing green of all my dreams,
   So I can see well like an old cat,
   So I can hear well like a big whale,
   So I can talk well like a huge tree.

   Bail me out, bail me out, bail me out
   Amazing fine green of all my dreams
   So I can be on full beam, on full beam,
   Bail me out, bail me out, bail me out,
   So I can reach Venus and dine with her.

Carrefour de beaucoup de bars

That day
The sun went to bed early enough
After warming *Carrefour de beaucoup de bars.*

And,

Like flies that often invade garbage cans
To feast on slimy, fetid juice oozing out of rot
They rushed to *Carrefour de beaucoup de bars*
The way decaying roots spread death to branches.

Like cockroaches that often invade dark kitchens
To feast on leftovers in uncovered abandoned dishes
They rushed to *Carrefour de beaucoup de bars*
The way mice overrun a corn barn.

Like sparrows that often dive into latrines
To feast on termites and greasy maggots
They rushed to *Carrefour de beaucoup de bars*
The way a hungry rattlesnake glides after its prey.

Like vultures that often swoop down
To feast on carrions left by wolves
They rushed to *Carrefour de beaucoup de bars*
The way dogs rush to the place they are fed.

In *Carrefour de beaucoup de bars*
Sheep have no choice when in the jaws of wolves.

In *Carrefour de beaucoup de bars*
Dogs and their puppies bark alike.

In *Carrefour de beaucoup de bars*
Every puppy is as fleshy as its mother.

In *Carrefour de beaucoup de bars*
Dogs wag their tails not for you, but for your food.

In *Carrefour de beaucoup de bars*
You sleep with dogs and rise with fleas.
And by the time the sun gets up from sleep
You are carried to the cemetery in the rain.

For Better and for Worse

Now it came about that darkness enveloped the earth
And animals shrieked in fright, like deer at crossroads,
And clung to each other, for better and for worse,
Till the sun would bow to let the eclipse pass.

And when the sky got clearer and clearer, like blossoming lilies,
The vows began to melt on their itchy lips like ice cubes in beer.
Doves began to call eagles names; hinds became bitches to bucks;
Cows and hens began to address bulls and cocks in borrowed robes.

Then, when the sun finally showed its true baldness
Bitches began to desert their kennels for want of food;
Wasps began to sleep with spiders for want of beds;
Slugs began to form leagues with snails for want of shells.

The eclipse gone, like hazy comets speeding through space,
Hungry ticks began to sleep and dine with noisy mosquitos,
Thirsty hawks began to make friends with crocodiles,
And vixens were seen in their wretched lairs no more.

It's for better and for worse that a bee seeks the rose
And it's in sickness and in health that they both live.
So long as the rose spreads its hot petals to welcome the bee
So long the bee would prick its ovule to reach its sweet nectar.

One Night in Heaven

Like a fresh brook flowing into a tiny cave
I moved into a dark crypt, silent as a lone cat.
In there, like a ripe cashew nut in a hard shell
Ready to sprout at the call of the blazing sun
I stood still, gazing at winding narrow paths:
The first one leading into lovely dark woods,
And the second leading up a steep mossy hill.

I chose the second, sought to know its legend,
And like a feeble fawn learning how to walk,
I took a small step, took another, took a third.
A bright light hung in a thick fog above the hill
Showing a high great wall with a tiny pink gate.
I toiled up the hill, slipped and fell three times.
A bearded-face stood at the gate, keys in hand.

I got in, having shed my skin like snakes do.
A huge golden dome stood at the lush yard's centre
Just like the large meeting houses in our royal palaces
In which chiefs sit in council with the land's greybeards
And listen to cases of all sorts, tabled by the common run -
Land issues, witchcraft, witch-hunting, libel, cheating, theft -
And pass sound judgements that bind the community together.

Surrounding the large golden dome were posh villas,
White, creamy, distancing themselves from one another
Like the ones in which several wives live in royal palaces.
Running splash of diamond, gold, silver and violet everywhere,
Multiple fine pillars of fizzy light glowed on the sleeping horizon,
Complex sounds of refreshing music enveloped the spicy air, and,
The captured air stood still, heavy with fragrant fresh garden scents.

Rays peeped out from beneath the dome, a mass of colours,
Revealing seven pillars of light surrounding a golden throne.
On the throne sat a sage, wool-like hair, snow white, hot eyes.
A cone stood on his round head, like that of an active volcano.
He sat like a fig tree that can't walk though its roots go very far
Clad in a lavish kingly garment, the type worn on coronation day.
A chief is hot fire, so we keep our distance when warming ourselves.

Choirs here, choirs there, left and right, choirs everywhere,
Some in white, some in cream, some in yellow, some in gold,
Jolly symphonies from the multiple choirs soothing the quiet air:
The soft sound of the fine piano, the calm pitch of the silver piccolo,
The deep timbre of guitar and violin strings and of drum membranes,
And the apt unison of flutes, trumpets, saxophones, xylophones in play
Transformed the restive man in me to a spirit cell in orbit to die no more.

Standing like an orphaned calf that licks its own back, in that orbit,
A sudden violet ray of blissful and inviting light glowed in front of me,
And it led me into a room of succulent joy, its air fresh as morning dew.
While in, I learned that cliffs become meadows when one is in true love.
While in, I learned that if a full moon loves you, why worry about the stars;
I learned that true love is like misty rain, coming softly but flooding the river;
Yes, I learned that true love, like rain, does not choose the grass on which it falls.

Take Me to Jerusalem

A dainty bitch laid by a cosy moor, deep dark,
Fresh like clear water meadows in the spring,
Ready to swan to the Jerusalem of its dreams
Like wood already touched by harmattan fire.

Since the way to a beloved is never ever thorny
A timber wolf swanned by, like a hungry kite,
And mounted on the waiting willing tiny bitch
Like a bushy starving fox on a vixen on heat.

It found in the graceful and welcoming bitch
A fine narrow straight path, shiny like porcelain,
Leading to Jerusalem, the land of peach nectar,
And it turned on the engine of its van, deftly.

The engine roared like a lion famished for weeks,
The wolf smashed the clutch, with clenched teeth,
Changed the gear, low to high, bottom to top, firmly,
And drove off wildly, crashing through the gears.

When the van pulled up with a screech of brakes,
The grinding of gears touching the bitch's spine,
The bitch shrieked, whispering "Yes! Yes! Come".
And the wolf murmured: "I'm coming! I'm coming!".

Yes come! Yes, come on! Take me to Jerusalem.
Yes! Yes, I'm getting there! Yes, I'm there! Yes!
And when the grinding gradually slowed down
The engine ceased. Thank you, thank you! *Ah*!

SEASON 4

ECSTASY

Eve at Birth

She came out of the stolid rib
Like a crafty vixen out of its lair
Poised to lull her man to Golgotha.

With skin as white as a ghost
No darkness filled her sick heart
The way soot fills a fierce furnace.

With a tongue as sharp as a blade
She tore the pointed ears of her man
And made him know the taste of nectar.

Ah sweet nectar, he mused, ah sweet nectar,
Hidden in golden lobes away from man
You make me know who I am: a man!

Eve at birth,
Beautiful like a well-crafted coffin,
Made her man know how good death is.

Lebong at Birth

Lebong,
You are welcome.
You are welcome to our family.
You are welcome to this household.
You are welcome to this beautiful world.
We welcome you with open hands, in good faith.
We know you have come to stay; we know you have.

Lebong,
The grass withers,
Flowers fade with passing time
But your beauty will stay forever
For God created you in the image of the star
And he has also set eternity in your youthful heart
So you may give this family more seeds for it the shine.

Lebong,
Cub of the homestead,
We have many things for you:
These are your kola nuts and palm oil;
These are your cashew nuts, salt and melon.
Male child, you will bring this family together
So that the giant rat will not dig this compound.

Lebong,
Reward of God,
You are like the fish in a pond
That always comes up to the surface
To tell us how many teeth the crocodile has.
Like a cockerel that crows not only for the household
You shall live to crow loud to wake up the entire village.

ML, the Fairest Flower from Cupid

Like a nascent meteor in a grey atmosphere
Making its pink line across a quiet night sky
As it sails through heavy nimbus clouds with ease
Settling firmly on a rocky stout dormant high volcano
You emerged gingerly from the bottom of deep ravines
And squinted your way deftly through bearded ebony skins,
To become the fairest flower ever known from Cupid's hands.

Fairest flower, the bluebell, the bulb, the daisy, and the lily
Are truly lost for ages in your stunning unfathomable legend;
The aster, the calla, the canna, the caper, the catkin and the mint
See you all the time like an incredibly graceful peacock among birds;
The fennel, the flax, the iris, the lilac, the lime, the mullein and the myrtle
Think you were fashioned with the gracious porcelain from Cupid's realm
The reason you are surely the fairest of flowers ever seen from that realm.

Fairest flower, bees scramble daily for your fine nectar
But you always stay stiff dumb like sleeping Alpine rocks;
Countless worms search all night for your bed of crimson joy
Not knowing that you are the buoyant morning glory ever known
That opens its petals in the morning and closes them in the afternoon.
Multitudes of lustful golden male crickets chirp endlessly around your ears
But you often block those copper ears of yours with solid wax from Heaven.
The rose does not brag about its rosiness, it simply blossoms as it does.
Yes, it blossoms well, unknown to itself, for the eye does not see itself.
Trees in full blossom spread their delicate fragrance in their surround-
ings

Surely for the benefit of those who truly care about fine scents in their lives.
Scents from seas and hills are not smelt by the seas and the hills themselves,
They are meant to soothe the multitude who care about their glorious presence,
They are not meant for themselves; they are meant for those who care about them.

Rose

Rose,
Of all the flowers I know
You stand out like a peacock among birds.
The peacock beats other birds in colour
You beat other flowers in elegance.
The elephant beats other animals in size
You beat other flowers in scent
The baobab beats other trees in height
You beat other flowers in look.

Rose,
Like a cockscomb on a cock's head
You stand out as graceful as a swan.
Like bright buttons on a duke's suit
You are as clear as crystal earrings.
Like the golden spots on the leopard
You are like confetti on a new couple.
Like a moon with its elegant crescents
You are a necklace of golden beads.
Like gold strings in a guitar
You are the jewel in the crown

But…
Tell me Rose, tell me,
The daisy is as fresh, the pansy as cool;
The lily is as cute, the tulip as soft;
The daffodil is as sweet, the clover as neat;
But why do bees seek only your own nectar? Why?
What manner of flower are you? Tell me, tell me.
Don't tell me you are the blooming cereus
That opens only at night.
Yes, don't tell me.
Don't.

The Last Virgin

There she stands, plump and fresh,
Like tomatoes glittering in a garden.
There she stands, radiant with health,
Like the turtle that lays a thousand eggs.
There she stands, with a radiant smile,
Like a newly wedded bride on a rostrum.
There she stands, with eyes and teeth
Radiant like the sun in a clear blue sky.
There she stands, sturdy, full of energy,
Like a bull that saves others from a pit.

And, like a camel that never sees its own hump,
She is like the farmer who never eats his fine grapes
Like patience that is the mother of a beautiful child
She is like the wise man whose heart lies quiet like limpid water.
Like the dog that eats bones because no one gives it meat
She is like the man who sees promises on the flat chest of a wench.
Like men who become wise when they begin to run out of money
She is like the sun that stores energy for yet another day.
Unlike the skin of a leopard that is beautiful and not its heart,
She is like a pool, beautiful on the surface and nice to swim in.

And, lo, she is a rock pool, fresh, lemon green surface glittering in the sun
Like fresh morning dew on cocoyam leaves, still to spill over.
And, lo, she is a rock pool, still, hemmed in and offering no relaxing place
For bees that scramble for nectar or fleas that settle on naked bodies.
Her ears are never standing like those of a rabbit
For she knows that beautiful words don't put porridge in the pot.
Unlike the chicken with beautiful plumage that does not sit in a corner

She is the bird with bright feathers always found in the nest.
Unlike the monkey that jumps from tree to tree for fruits
She is the patient dog that longs for the fattest bone.

SEASON 5

FULFILMENT

First Rains

They sweep in like battalions of invading warring locusts
Munching on every single green on vast blossoming fields
Leaving tantalised herds of cattle licking their red wounds.

They sound like the brisk roars of angry widowed lion kings
Wandering across open moorlands for several mating seasons
Eager to quench the flames raging through their iron joysticks.

Like a faithful dog that won't leave its owner to follow a king
First rains never leave the hot Earth to seek Jupiter the most high
They always seek to cool the Earth like joyous old dik-diks in love.

First rains always come with their own water and so respect no one.
He who always carries his own water is never hit by some raging thirst.
The water that first rains always carry is real manna from its own very rock.

It always floods the hot Earth like huge waves breaking on dry shores
It penetrates every single hole in the sun-baked soil like worms in sloughs
Leaving the tired soil pregnant with a million tadpoles to sustain the Earth.

Half Widows

Like hapless wax in a fiery oven
The tired bulls melted in turns.
Like dry leaves in the open Sahel
They surrendered to a blazing fire.

Like mice spared by an angry house fire
The merry cows now swing pass, one by one,
With cockscombs on their unshaven heads
Like night birds on a fashion show at noon.

Like those who drink from River Lethe
They resurface in style in the wide ranch
Having lost count of bygone good days
When sweethearts swam in fresh pools.

Single bulls in the fine ranch welcome some
With open arms like the mouth of crocodiles;
Those with known partners welcome the others
With chests as wide as the ears of an elephant.

Parading the fields clad in colours of the rainbow,
Arm in arm like cockroaches in a hot love dance
They wag their tails and wiggle their fleshy hips
Chanting praises to the god of fire, the Highest.

Joy-stick

Stiff,
Seeking
Direction &
Landing zone
On the conical
Control tower,
Veins strained.
What flows
In the mind
Flows in the stick.
What the mind wants
The stick wants as well:
The joy of fondling well
The joy of searching deep
The joy of pounding deep
The joy of seeking sweets
The joy of sucking sweets
The joy of staying good
The joy of feeling good
The joy of sowing
The joy of reaping
When the labour
Is over,
Well
Over.

Love Letter

Rose,
Of all the flowers I know in the universe
You stand out like a peacock among birds.
The peacock beats all other birds in colour
And you beat all other flowers in elegance.

Rose,
The daisy is as fresh, asters & iris as cool;
The daffodil is as cute, lily & tulip as soft;
The peony is as sweet, calla & clover as neat;
But it is only your nectar that bees can suck.

Rose,
Amazing gel, what else shall I compare you to?
I gasp for words; I have no other words for you,
Your radiance blurs the wide lexicon in my mind.
At first I thought I was truly blind, though I see well.

Rose,
How lucky is the bat to share the night with the owl!
Sure, there is no darkness where there is ardent love
For the heat each person generates brightens the night
And ignites the love gas leaking from each other's heart.

Rose,
You are not like the ripe grapes we see by the roadside
For those grapes are for the harvest of ravening wolves.
You are not like the dull fish that fell in love with a bird
For you know that the two cannot build a home together.

Rose,
You and I are like the yam and the knife of the homestead
For there is nothing in yams that the knife does not know.
You and I are like the tortoise and its God-given carapace
For the tortoise does not embark on a journey without it.

Rose
Like the lion that does not look back when it is after its prey
So too shall I not look back in this journey ordained by Cupid.
Like a monkey that won't leave her baby to fall from a branch
So too shall I not leave you to fall from Mount Kilimanjaro.

Taboo Love

Is it for lack of cows on a farm
That a bull should marry his mother?
Cows of the cattle type roam the fields
Like a bunch of Wags roam streets at night.
Those of the elephant type, open as day,
Are always there to lift one to blissful realms.
Those of the seal type loiter far in dark waters
With arched fleshy hips like humps of camels.
And those of the whale type comb the ocean
As fierce bitches on heat comb towns for dogs.

Yes, this bull, like a self-pollinated bush flower
Perched on a barren hilltop in an open dry savannah,
Mounted on his mother's back, hands up, feet down,
Like a kangaroo about to hop when it senses danger.
What manner of man graduates from his mother's breast
Then seeks her nectar the way bees seek that of the rose?
When a river is thirsty, does it drink its own water?
When a flea cannot find blood, does it drink water?
When a lion cannot find meat, does it eat grass?
If love is a sickness, common sense is the remedy.

SEASON 6

RAVENING

Dating

Dating a scammer:
Baby, I'm hungry.
I will MoMo you.

Dating a lawyer:
Baby, I'm hungry.
Do you have evidence?

Dating a teacher:
Baby, I'm hungry.
Please, I'm still in class.

Dating a politician:
Baby, I'm hungry.
Who did you vote for?

Dating a classmate:
Baby, I'm hungry.
Expecting money soon.

Dating a policeman:
Baby, I'm hungry.
I will soon go to the road.

Dating a cashier:
Baby, I'm hungry.
Let me balance my records.

Dating a footballer:
Baby, I'm hungry.
Waiting for our bonuses.

Dating a manager:
Baby, I'm hungry.
Stop being careless with money.

Dating a traditional doctor:
Baby, I'm hungry.
Try African panacea.

Dating,
What is it?
Is it life for real?

March 8

My gas don finish.
Finish how? When? Hein?
This morning. Was frying eggs.
How many daddies do you fry for?
Whetti? Hmm abeg, abeg, no miooh!

A man is like a well in the Sahel, abi?
How is that? How? A well? tell me how.
Cos it dries up fast when visited too often.
Daddy, make quick abeg. Airtime …. airtime!
Ah, no longer gas! Hmm. It's airtime now, abi?

So, you call what you sent to me last night airtime?
How many calls did you make last night? How many?
Cheiiiiii! What do you mean? Hein? What do you mean?
Gas, airtime, iPhone, rents, soon it will be the eagle's eggs.
Abeg, daddy I'm running out of airtime. Please call me back.

Men of God

From open fissures in a vast wilderness
Emerged arachnids with syringe-like tongues
Poised to inject litanies of healing ramblings
Into ears unused to angelic melodies and grace.

Wuna hear!

Cream-coated,
The ramblings are said to be the ageless doctrines
Of a long-forgotten healing God of all maladies:
From toe fungi through itchy anuses to head rashes.

Wuna hear!

Sugar-coated,
The ramblings are said to be placed in the mouth of augurs
Meant to show the sick the way to God's lovely doorstep
While shunning graveyards in which our forebears repose.

Wuna hear!

Then came the first Man of God, cast away by Mulungu,
In bright suits or trousers and long-sleeve shirts most of the time,
Finely polished shoes to match, well-cut hair, and gold finger rings,
He jabbed his flock in the ears with stories of sin and damnation.

Wuna hear!

And then the second Man of God, defected from Nyame's party,
As if on cue, appeared on stage like a mad bear with a sore head,
Ranted about the wages of sin, God's whip and the scourge of hell,
Quoting from the Revelation and the Seven Books of Moses.

Wuna hear!

And then the third Man of God, supposed fire-eater in Nun's realm,
Bald as a coot, jumped in like a baboon fleeing from a hail of arrows,
Talked about devils on the cross, gazing at polygamists in the gathering,
And chanted the Beatitudes, his hands hanging like the wings of a bat.

Wuna hear!

And then the fourth Man of God, Olodumare's renegade timekeeper,
Swaggered in like a gorilla, looking merry and happy with himself,
Like a lone bull in a herd of cows, sniffing at asses here and there.
Preaching, he was like a great fire that erupts with tiny sparks.

Wuna hear!

And then the fifth Man of God, Nzambi's deranged enfant terrible,
A rattlesnake for Satan's converts, a cat for mice, a cock for weevils,
Mounted the podium, with 'Holy Ghost Fire' in his watery mouth,
Recited Mark 9:43 and talked fiercely about Sodom and Gomorrah.

Wuna hear fine fine!

Yes, listen carefully. Listen with the ears of a bat, not those of a squid,
Ears that do not listen to advice accompany the head when chopped off.
Listen, listen well, listen, a fool and water go the way they are diverted.
Listen, listen, listen, no one drinks medicine on behalf of a sick person.

Wuna hear fine fine!

Birds sing not because they have answers but because they have songs,
Cardinals sing in the morning, common nightingales sing all night long

Kites and larks sing while flying, robins and sparrows while perching
But it's not because the lizard nods its head that means it's in agreement.
Wuna hear fine fine!

Symptoms

Deafness…
Daddy, didn't you hear your phone ring?
I called when tapeworms seized my intestines.
Baby, I was reading the tale of your life with bees.

Excuses…
Baby, can we meet in Jupiter this weekend?
Waves will bring salmon to the beach for roasting.
Daddy, the moon hasn't finished crossing the town.

Blindness…
Daddy, didn't you see my messages?
I was frying eggs when the bottle ran out of gas
Baby, the war in Ukraine is still raging on, you know?

Always busy…
Baby, why didn't you pick my calls?
Needed to know when bees usually seek nectar.
Daddy, I was counting the number of stars in the sky.

Always on mission…
Daddy, why not take me to Oasis on my birthday?
Truly, I long to reach Jerusalem while we are there.
Baby, I'll be going to Mars to learn how eclipses come about.

And the symptoms hung on like ticks on dogs
Leaving the Anansi-Chameleon bond fade away
Like a weary rainbow fading from a midnight sky.

Valentine Gift

Babe!
Yes babe.
Valentine is around the corner ooh.
Valentine? Who is he? How close?
Around the corner. Not far. Nearby.
Let him come in then. Beckon him.
Hope you are getting ready, Babe.
Ready for what? Who is he to us?

Babe, truly, it's like you're kidding!
Kidding? How? Is he taking us out?
Valentine, taking you and I out, sha?
Yes, or is the man here for you alone?
Abeg, I need my Valentine gift today.
Ha, today! Need a gift for my combi, abi?
No no! Abeg, na me bi your combi. Na me.
So, who bi dis your Valentine? Who bi he?

SEASON 7

ENTREATIES

Before You Sleep

Before you sleep
Sweep the coops
Sweep before your fowls learn to strut
Lest they grow up and live with lice.
For he who lives with lice
Will go with lice.

Before you sleep
Sweep the kennels
Sweep before your dogs learn to run
Lest they grow up and live with fleas.
For he who lives with fleas
Will go with fleas.

Before you sleep
Sweep your yard
Sweep before your kids learn to walk
Lest they grow up and live with bugs.
For he who lives with bugs
Will go with bugs.

Before you sleep
Share a path with someone
Share a path as you wander in the woods
Lest you jump from tree to tree like apes.
For the ape that jumps from tree to tree
Is the harvest of the wily fox.

Before you sleep
Share a dream with someone
Share a dream before you sleep
Lest the lion in you be turned to a sheep.

For an army of sheep led by a lion
Can defeat an army of lions led by a sheep.

GHS Mamfe

From the banks of the graceful Manyu
Eerie cries rend crimson skies
As bees rend daisies for sweet nectar
The way rodents rend sacks for corn.

GHS Mamfe,
Lying by the graceful Manyu
In whose welcoming water
Alligators herald the crocodile
While turtles sleep with an eye open.

GHS Mamfe,
Lying by the graceful Manyu,
In whose welcoming water
Hippopotami bellow commands
While oysters take shelter in their caves.

GHS Mamfe,
Lying by the graceful Manyu,
On whose welcoming banks
Adders glide in graceful elegance
In search of ducks' juicy eggs.

GHS Mamfe,
Lying by the graceful Manyu,
On whose welcoming banks
Goats, with wagging tails,
Go for sweet potato vines.

GHS Mamfe,
In whose fine classrooms
Kids tussle for knowledge

The way kittens scramble
For their mother's milk.

GHS Mamfe,
In whose fine laboratories
Kids juggle for life's panacea
The way a lively orchestra
Plays with great panache.

GHS, GHS, our lovely GHS,
Birds sing on every fruit tree around
While dogs dance in every household
The field is full of grasshoppers in parallel lines
And the praying mantis keeps praying in the woods.

GHS, GHS, does it occur to the vulture
That sparrows chirp and swallows twitter
But they share the same field peacefully?
GHS, our GHS, does it occur to the crocodile
That frogs and toads look really different
But they share the same swamp peacefully?

GHS, our lovely GHS, let vampire bats know
That it is not because one has been stung by a bee
That should make him destroy all beehives.

GHS, our lovely GHS, let vampires know
That the absence of tigers should not make
The wildcat very self-important.
Be steadfast, GHS, be steadfast,
A fox is not as swift as a hare
But, prowling, its traps pay off a hundredfold.

Be steadfast, GHS, be steadfast,
A fig tree cannot walk, but its roots go very far.
He who overcomes rain is not worried about the dew.

Money or Grammar?

Money without grammar is a shortcut;
No shortcuts exist to the top of a palm tree.
Grammar without money is pidgin;
No pidgin is spoken on Wall Street.

Money without grammar is darkness.
If money were to be kept by mosquitoes
Many would spend the night with them.

Money without grammar is dirt.
If money were to be kept in dustbins
Many would become scavengers.

Money without grammar is a monkey.
If money were to be kept up in trees
Many would be married to monkeys.

Grammar, even without money, is rain.
Like rain, it fertilises the soil
And enables plants to green the earth.

Grammar, even without money, is love.
Like love, it is misty rain,
It comes softly but floods a river.

Grammar, even without money, is a stream.
Like a stream, it doesn't forget its origin
However far it flows.

Money flies off the earth and lands on an anthill.
Grammar flies off the earth and lands on an iroko.
Who is still on the ground: Money or Grammar?

One Eye

Hello berry
How are u today?
What's up, my berry?

Hi, kicking, like giraffes.
Kicking for survival,
And u my sherry?

Just there ooh, my berry,
But can't kill myself sha,
I want to get my lashes done.

Go ahead na? Any wahala?
Any wahala sherry, any wahala?
The day is still like a day-old chick.

But my money is not complete.
Lashes are something else now.
Need 10k more; 10k will help.

Do one eye, do one.
For a difference, do one eye.
Who else do you want to see you?

Difference how, me a cyclops, abi?
Like toucans among crows, abi?
How is that, abi, how is that?

Abeg do one eye, abeg, one eye.
Your purse is enough for one eye.
And one eye is good for me, do one.

Wartime Ladies

Thunder spoke on hilltops
And lightning pierced through the quiet sky.
Then, then … the sky was red with flying bullets
And grey fell and enveloped the town.

The Gracious Doves gathered in the town square, these ladies,
Some with leaves of nkeng, some with white handkerchiefs,
Some beckoning to the weary sun, some kneeling in prayer,
All summoning warlords to the town hall
Telling them that one cannot put out fire with fire.

Mmmmmmmmh! Who born dog?
Who tell dem say dis warlord dem get ear?
All man de sing i own song; sing i own wahala.
Est-ce que dis warlord dem de hear place sef?
Abeg, dis warlord dem ear don lock well well.

The Gentle Dams gathered at a road junction, these other ladies,
Some in black, some in red, all carrying fresh palm fronds,
Calling the warlords to see what the war has done
To see what fire has done to nests and sent birds fleeing.
To see what the hurricane has done to a million egg baskets.

Éeh kiiiiiiiiiiiié! Bébélé Zamba!
Who tell dem say warlord dem get eye?
Est-ce que war get eye sef?
All man cover i face with anyang pot
Like say dem want dance mbagalum dance.

The Butterflies flit in and out of town, these ones,
These ones who don't want to be called 'mama',
Willing to answer the call of loins, to put out fire,

Knowing that when your house is gripped by fire
You don't choose who to help you put out the fire.

Cheiiiiiii! If moon like you for night
Weti you go do when sun komot for day time?
Chameleon de change i colour for match with ground
Ground no de change colour for match with chameleon
Abi?

Then came The Cream Ladies, the champagne drinkers,
With their rhetoric; with their love rhetoric on their lips:
"If the full moon loves you, why worry about the stars?"
They paraded the streets like an army of sheep led by a lion
That is not brave enough to tell the lion that its breath smells.

Haba!!! Wuna tell me.
Love fit make man forget say rain de fall?
Love fit make man leave mosquito sing for i ear?
Love fit make mami-fowl forget say hawk de for bush?
Abeg, wuna no make me laugh.

The Daisies, who can't be won over even with elephant tusks,
Those with the breasts you can't desire if your purse is empty,
Came and spoke with the tongue of an owl, hooting out their minds:
"A fight between grasshoppers is a joy to the crow;
A sheep does not lament the death of a goat's kid".

Komot me for deh, kuba-kuba demoiselle dem!
Est-ce que horse rider dem de stand when dog dem de bark?
If you no stand up for something you go fall down for something.
Tomorrow belong for people weh dem prepare for'am today.
No medicine fit cure bad-heart; no grass for bush fit fix palava.

SEASON 8

RIPPLES

Massa Talk-Talk Dem

For dis palava
Massa Talk-Talk dem de kind by kind.

Some de talk like parrot.
Dem talk like say dem no get dia own head.
When sheep talk, dem talk like sheep;
When rat talk, dem talk like rat;
When fox talk, dem talk like fox;
When snake talk, dem talk like snake.

Some de talk like say
Dem pump dia belly with lie-lie talk.
Dem see cat, dem call'am tiger;
Dem see wolf, dem call'am dog;
Dem see dove, dem call'am hawk;
Dem see locust, dem call'am grasshopper.

For before
We papa dia drum no de talk lie.
Dem born pikin, drum go talk de kind pikin;
Some man die, drum go talk de kind man;
Trinja come town, drum go talk de kind trinja;
Trouble enter town, drum go talk de kind trouble.

Today, cock i crow, Massa Talk-Talk say i bin caw;
Today, crow i caw, Massa Talk-Talk say i bin crow;
Today, bee i hum, Massa Talk-Talk say i bin drone;
Today, beetle i drone, Massa Talk-Talk say i bin hum.
Which one we go hear?
Which one we go tek'am?

Fowl de lay eggs
Snake too de lay eggs.
We fit say egg na egg
So make we chop snake i eggs?
We fit say so?
Wuna tell me.

Night Waka

When you want catch black goat for night
First take time look yi well well for day time
If no bi so, you no go fit catch'am for night.

You fit set trap catch rat mole for night
If for day time you no first know road for yi hole?
You fit?

Dis night waka weh some people dem de waka,
Weh dem de waka for beat other man weh dem no like,
Dis kind night waka de make sleep finish for my head.

No man want first see how other man de look for day time,
No man want first see weti other man de carry for day time,
No man want first see road weh other man pass for day time.

Wonda de so so happen inside thick bush for night time.
Weti weh all kind beef dem never see'am?
Weti weh all kind stick dem never hear?

Each time weh day break
Dis people dem de pass like say dem no bin chop for night time.
Dem de pass like people weh dem want go for Heaven meet God.

Njakri Tok

Man,
Shut up your mop ya.
Woman de house de pass you.
You deh here de tok like parrot
Krukrukrukrukrukrukrukrukru
Drink your mimbo go sleep fo house.
Drink go sleep fo your woman yi back.
When woman pas you, carry yi handbag ya.

Look yi,
Waka waka thing like dog.
Me a get woman fo house ya.
You de waka kunya kunya upside,
Kunya kunya fo nyung girl dem back,
Like fowl wey yi loss road fo night time.
Man weh yi make combi with nyung girl dem
Nyung girl weh dem fit be their pikin dem age
Hi go so so waka tok fo himself like craze man ya.

Ripples in the Pond

A warm breeze rippled the pond
The rippling water rippled fishes to the surface
And canoes rippled through the water for a catch.

The sound of rippling water
Alerted sparrow hawks, always in wait
Of rippling to the pond's surface for inspection.

The canoes rippled back
Leaving the rippling water to the birds
And were welcomed with rippling laughter.

Water rippled under the dock
Like the rippling of a lion's muscles
As welcoming laughter rippled through the air.

The ripple of laughter didn't last for long
As news rippled outward about an impending doom
From sparrow hawks that rippled back asking for accounts.

WhatsApp Chats

She lives off campus. Paradise City.
Perched on the southern fringe of the city –
Away from prying eyes.
No qualms.

Gud mrnx d. How was ur nite?
Gd monx baby. Calm. And urs?
Feverlike. U don troway me na? Long time
U said u lost ur phone, that's why
Was exptx u to buy me anoda one na?
Didn't tell me baby
Mmmmmmmmh. Who else is there?
Who knows? Wuna de lose phone with each new man
Hihihi. U funny

Tonite at GALAXY, not so?
What time d?
Pick u up at 10
Ok d. But need to do my hair. Need 10k for it
Ok. Thru ur mobile money?
Yep. Add anoda 20 for rubbx oil n perfume. They're finished
That makes 30k then?
Yes d. But round it up to 50. Need a dress n pair of shoes
No prob.

Hello baby, about to leave for urs. It's 9:30
Hello d. Mmmmmmmmh. Abeg let's leave it 4 nx wk
Nx wk? How? What de mata
Dat thg came ooh. In de hair salon. Maybe bc of de heat.
Which thing?
Redness. Abeg nx wk if u're around.

Hello baby. Gd monx.
Gud mrnx d. Are u back? Mmmh. Up to 2 wks?
Yeah, 2 wks. Much work. Returned last nite.
Hope u brought much thgs 4 ur baby. Waitx.

Hello d. Been waitx 4 too long na
Hello. Was busy with office work n stuff. See u at 7
No. Just stepped out. Ashia. Leave de thgs with Amy
Ok. So when?
Will call u ASAP

Hello baby. I've been waitx 4 long
4 what d
Ur call
Ok. I know d
U know?
Yes. Only dat de moon has not yet finished crossx de town.

SEASON 9

REVOLT

Dis War Sef

Dis war sef.
Lion i roar, some people dem roar with'am.
Hyena i scream, some people dem scream with'am.
Wolf i howl, some people dem howl with'am.
All man wan go palapala field
For fight for i own man.

Man soldier dem carry spear
Pikin soldier dem carry cutlass
Woman soldier dem carry knife
Book soldier dem carry android phone.

For palapala field all man say i de win:
Lion people say dem de win;
Hyena people say dem de win;
Wolf people say dem de win.

But bush de smell pass cat i shit
Lion people dem lie everywhere,
Hyena people dem lie everywhere,
Wolf people dem lie everywhere.
Who go carry who?
Who go bury who?

Facebook de talk i own talk for dey,
WhatsApp de talk i own talk for dey,
YouTube de talk i own talk for dey.
Dis Commander bin die last year, dis year i de shout command;
Dis Colonel bin die last week, dis week i de talk for radio;
Dis General die yesterday, today i de marry new wife.

Dis war sef
Why we no bin throw water for small spark when i start?
See now de big fire wey i don swallow palapala field.
Who go quench de fire now before i burn we all?
Cockroach know how for sing and dance for day time
But na fowl de prevent'am for sing and dance.
Wisdom be like mboma tree; no one man fit embrace'am.
Make fowl leave cockroach make i sing and dance;
Make all man sit under mboma tree, join hand and embrace'am.

He Ascended into Hell

In the small hours of that blissful morning
The rainbow hung high in the crimson sky,
Colourful bands of dancing cold cirrus clouds
Shading it from the view of the waking earth,
And some weight of air pulling the clouds away
Like waves pushing invading sea water onshore.

Just before dawn, when crickets chirp no more,
The time when icy dew begins to settle on grass,
When gummy sleep is about to leave heads alone,
The rooster chimed the notes of the morning song,
Summoning all the animals to the meeting ground,
Telling them that rising early makes the road short.

A thick dark cloud hung over the vast meeting ground
Like huge masses of unripe cones on feeble palm trees.
All the animals filed in like soldier ants, one after the other
And took their designated seats on the meeting's vast square.
The Lamb, the outspoken Secretary of the Council of Animals,
Got up, with fire in his eyes, read out the sole item on the agenda.

The assembled animals, roused to fever pitch, held their breath,
Anxiously waiting for the sentence passed on H.E. Leopard the Great
Who had been crushing all dissident animals during his iron-fist rule
Like crazy, vile, villainous and injurious waves breaking on the shore
Not knowing for sure that a well-knit jungle is stronger than a hammer.
The limpid air stood still, quiet as a mouse, silent as a country churchyard.

The sentence, when it came, fell like tornados ripping through multiple islands:

"For having betrayed the huge confidence placed on him by the people,
For having gaged the peoples' enquiring mouths these several seasons,
For having slaughtered our people in his dark secret abattoirs of shame,
For having made us paupers and having made our children flee the land,
Mr Leopard is henceforth dethroned and sentenced to death by being burnt alive."

Early that fateful morning, a distant star gleamed with delight in the dark-blue sky.
The time when sluggish sleep was slowly leaving the heads of animals in the colony
H.E. Leopard the Great of the Royal Colony was brought into the crematory chamber,
Hands handcuffed behind his back, legs firmly tied, and thrown into the flaming furnace.
Curious onlookers, with gleeful eyes, shrieked with laughter as his ashes rose to the sky,
And they all screamed with excitement: YES he has ascended into hell, this mad king.

Pikin Soldier Dem

For dis war
Pikin soldier dem plenty pass mark.
Pikin weh dem no know book, dem deh dey;
Boy pikin weh dem de still piss for bed, dem deh dey;
Girl pikin weh dem never start see dia moon, dem deh dey.

For camp
Dem rub girl pikin dem with lavinda
Dem tie jigidja for dia neck and waste
Dem show dem de kind bed weh big massa dem de sleep
And de kind chop weh big massa dem de chop.

For camp
Dem cut boy pikin dem skin
And rub dem with odeishi.
Dem put some for dia eye
Dem put some for dia mouth
Dem tie red and black cloth for dia skin
And dem give dem gun for carry.

For palapala field
Boy pikin dem carry gun weh i big pass dem
Dem carry gun weh i heavy pass dem
And dem follow dia massa dem
Like sheep pikin dem de follow dia mami for bush.

For palapala field boy pikin soldier
Dem waka like dog weh i no get tail
Dem waka like hunter man i dog weh i no know bush
Dem waka like cow weh i de go for butcher house
Dem waka like swine weh i no know say lion too de for bush.

Small time dem hear big big noise bum bum bum
Like say some big mboma tree don fall for bush
Like say thunder don broke some big mountain
Dem chakara like pikin fowl dem weh dem see hawk
Dem chakara like cockroach dem weh dem see fire.

"You, take dis side; you, take dat side, quick quick",
"Surround de enemy, faya to faya, faya to faya, fayaaa",
Big massa pass command. Fayaaaaaaaa, fayaaaaaaaa
Kriiik kriik kriik buuuum; Kriiik kriik kriik buuuum
Fayaaaaaaaa, fayaaaaaaaa; Kriiik kriik kriik buuuum

When day break, people see say war no get eye
Soldier for dis side dem die like fowl for sick time
Soldier for dat side dem die like fish for dry land
Pikin soldier dem die pass grass for dry season.
Mm. Man weh i sleep with dog dem go wek'up with tick dem.

Shithole

Shithole?
Did we hear well?
Mmmmmmmmh!
Shithole indeed!

How did you see our shitholes
From where you perch across the Atlantic?
You must be using some binoculars
To see, smell and clean our shitholes
That your predecessors did not have.
But you have to be careful to kill a fly
That is perched on someone's scrotum.

Tell us.
Are there shitholes across the Pacific?
Tell us, can your binoculars spot any?
Or are lands across the Pacific deep wells?
You know, when a needle falls into a deep well
Few will be able to see it.
You may be one of those few.

Tell us
The way our shitholes look like
Since a camel cannot see its own hump.
Tell us; tell us.
Do they look like golf holes?
Are there fairways around the holes?
Are they as hairy as putting greens?

Tell us.
If the throat swallows a knife
The anus must find a way of expelling it, isn't it?

Can the mouth teach the shithole how to expel a knife?
Does the crocodile's mouth have the power of its tail?
Can the mouth fart to relief someone of pain?
Tell us; can it?

You know what?
Until hawks have their historians
Tales of the hunt shall always glorify eagles.
Both soar high above the tallest of trees
Both glide through the air in shine and rain
Both swoop depending on their kind of winds
And they have their stories true to their kind.

You know what?
Every bear has its den, as every worm has its hole.
In a bear's eyes, all things belong to the bear.
In a worm's eyes, the earth belongs to the worm.

Wood Power

The wood was vast, lovely, dense and deep
Animal families had their trails and tongues
Monkeys chattered, hyenas screamed
Elephants trumpeted, snakes hissed
Tigers growled, rats squeaked
Wolves yelled, cats purred
Lions roared, deer belled
Cattle bellowed
Foxes yelped
Kangaroos
Chortled
Kittens
Mewed.
Each
Bird
Family
In the wood
Had its own song
True to its kind and style
And they sang with ease and style.

Then the tortoise crawled in with his big sense
He crawled in gingerly with a sweet tongue
Saying he could speak like each animal
And could sing like each bird kind
The reason why he should be king
Of the wood and ruler of all
And handed the royal cup
Of command to hold.
Once handed to him
He asked each one
To talk or sing
And he echoed
Each of them
Asking them
To henceforth
Talk and sing like him.
The wood rose to its feet
Seized the cup, fought him
And threw him on his back.

SEASON 10

STARLIGHT

Andong's Tongue

Njong,
My husband,
Son of a chief,
Son of the lion,
The lion that prowls
The woods unchallenged
Like the eagle among birds.
You came to my father's compound
You came to looked for me; yes you did.
I did not come to look for you; I did not.
I did not ask you to marry me; I did not.
Does a girl ever ask a man to marry her?
Where will she hide her head in the land?
Will she ever appear on the dancing arena?
Will she ever appear in the village market?
Will she ever join her mother in the kitchen?

Njong,
My chief,
You came for me.
You came on your own
Like a hunter to in the wild;
Like a hunter looking for game.
And you fell on my father's feet
Like a hungry cub before its mother
Eager to suck at its mother's breast.
When my dear father gave his consent
When he accepted you to be my husband
Did I refuse? Did I? How could I refuse?
Who has ever refused her father's choice?
Where will she find the mouth to say so?
Chicks eat where they're beckoned to eat.
Dogs eat where they're beckoned to eat.

Njong,
My man,
The noble one,
I accepted you.
I accepted you with one heart.
I believed you came with one heart.
I have heated water for your evening bath,
I have cooked porridge and you have eaten,
I have carried fresh water to quench your thirst,
I have warmed your bed these several seasons.
You have always assigned me by day and night.
I've given you the sons & daughters you longed for.
Have I ever given you hot water to drink? Have I?
Have I ever given you raw cocoyam to eat? Have I?
And now you behave towards the one you begged for
Like a fierce hunter who is tracking an elephant.
Njong,

My lion,
Lord of the forest.
Love is like a baby;
It needs to be treated tenderly.
A husband may be the head of a home
But the wife is the real heart of the homestead.
Know that a cockroach knows how to sing and dance
But it is the hen that prevents it from performing its art.
It cannot perform its art during the day because of the hen.
You are the hen in the colony of cockroaches. Yes you are.
True, a cockroach cannot sing and dance in this compound.
How can it when the hen in you is as deadly as the king cobra?
Know that the cockroach in this compound is now a rattle snake.
If you provoke a rattlesnake, you must be prepared to be bitten by it.
Know that a flea can trouble a lion more than a lion can trouble a flea.

Tale Time

Each day, songbirds chime the notes of parting day
Crickets chirp weary ants into their tiny holes
Grey clouds send goats packing into their fold
The fading sun sends fowls strutting to their coop
Hooting owls send ducks waddling to their barn
And a piercing star sends birds flying off the earth
Giving way to tale time.

At tale time
The household sits up
Like quiet mice waiting for the barn owner to sleep
As mom arranges her ant-infested faggots
And fans the feeble flames under the iron pot
For the evening meal to get ready on time
Lest dad starts screaming like a hungry hyena.

At tale time
The household sits up
In wait for the evening meal
Alert like geckoes eager to catch their prey
Still like a contented cat purring on its owner's lap
Poised like apes basking in the mid-day sun
As dad lies stretched out on his cane chair.

At tale time
We test our wits with riddles of the land
To lay the ground for the hatching of tales
For a blunt machete cannot fell an iroko tree
Neither can the sun claim it has power over the moon
Since it cannot shine and light our hills at night.

At tale time
For meals of days ahead
Our nails are heard busy peeling beans
Little sticks are heard undoing melon pods
Like birds with tails heard squawking
Or rabbits squealing over blades of grass.

Having eaten to his fill
Dad gulps down a few horns of palm wine
To wash his throat
Having eaten to our fill
Mom and us drink spring water
To wash our throats.

Having washed our throats
The household listens with ears of a rabbit,
Akamin, my brother, sitting same side with dad
And Ngeh, my sister, on the same side with mom.
Mom takes the floor and narrates tales of the land
Cooing like a dove emerging from a shrub.

Mom: My house has no door. What is it?
Ngeh: An egg. An egg has no door.
Mom: That's right.
Do you know why hawks catch chicks?
Ngeh: No. Tell us so that we may also know.
Mom: A cock and a hen caught and ate Mr. Cricket,
The doctor who went to heal the hawk's baby,
And the baby died for lack of treatment.
From that day hawks swore to take revenge on chickens
That is why they prey on their young ones.
Ngeh: That serves them right, foolish creatures.

Akamin: Animals, like men, dig their own graves.
I hear the hen and the hawk had another problem…
The hen had accepted a marriage proposal from the hawk
But she overturned her decision at the last minute.
In retaliation, the hawk decided to be killing chicks.

This is what I heard. Is that true?
Mom: The chicken never wins in a court of hawks.
Just like in birds' court, a cockroach never wins his case.
Do goats have a voice in an assembly of hyenas?
When the hyena is a judge, the goat has no rights.
So, one should never rub bottoms with a porcupine.
Ngeh: You have said it all, mom. We get you.
Eggs should not dance with stones.
Mom: Yes. The butterfly that brushes against thorns
Will end up tearing its wings.

Mom: I am here and I am there. Who am I?
Akamin: The sun. The sun is here and there.
Mom: That's not true.
Akamin: Then tell us so that we may also know.
Mom: Give me a chief.
Akamin: I give you Chief Nyase of Mbalangong
Mom: I don't know him. Give me a renown chief.
Akamin: I give you chief Mbia the Third of Nyaka
Mom: Yes, I accept. That is a brave chief, a lion king.
Do you know why people die?
Akamin: Tell us so that we may also know.
Mom: Ndem, having created human beings,
Decided that they should live as long as a rock,
Like Nchiangong rock overlooking River Nzefeh,
Saying that they should never experience death.
He sent the dog to convey this message to people
The dog spent time on the way hunting for rodents.
Ndem then changed his mind and sent the chameleon.
The chameleon bypassed the dog unnoticed
And announced the death message to mankind.
This is why human beings do not live for ever
Like Nchiangong rock overlooking River Nzefeh.

The household heaved a sigh, all looking like lost calves.
Akamin: Mom, can a rooster crow for the whole world?
Mom: A rooster shouldn't allow its belly to make it useless

The dog allowed its belly to make it useless to mankind.
Eat when the food is ready and speak at the right time.

As the night dragged on and the moon became brighter
And words became sweeter and sweeter like fresh wine
Ears stood on end, like those of a silent cat on mice hunt,
Waiting for more good grains to fill the waiting baskets.

Mom: I have another story for your ears
Akamin: Let us hear it.
Mom: Who knows how animals got their colour?
Akamin: I don't know. Tell us.
Ngeh: I know.
Akamin: Then tell us so that we may also know.
Ngeh: Give me a chief, an important chief.
Akamin: I give you Chief Kuchala of Aposa
Ngeh: I don't like him. He is a greedy chief.
He is not different from a green mamba
His greed is like that of a green mamba
Who wants to swallow an elephant.
Akamin: Then I give you Chief Abasoba of Mbacham
Ngeh: I accept. I like him. He is not the kind of chief
Who asks whether a leopard is a male or a female
When one is chasing us from its hiding place in the bush.
So here comes my story on how animals got their colour.
The meerkat said if any animal in the bush killed a buck
And bring the meat to him, he will paint a colour on him.
The hyena killed a buck, ate all the meat himself
And took the fleshless bones to the meerkat.
The meerkat said "Kneel down".
The hyena knelt down, like a stubborn child,
And the meerkat painted ugly marks on him.
The meerkat then said to all the other animals
"If anyone cheats me, I will do the same to him".
The leopard went out hunting and killed a buck
And brought it to the meerkat whole, unskinned,
The meerkat told the leopard to sit down
He sat down like a child for a father's blessing

And the meerkat painted him a beautiful colour
Saying, with the authority of he who owns the world
"If anyone keeps his words with me, I will do the same to him"
This is how all animals got their colour from the meerkat.

Dad: The hyena was foolish and too full of himself
Wisdom does not come overnight, it is like misty rain
Coming slowly but filling the river at the end of the day.
It is like fire; people take it from others to their homes.
The hyena emptied his heart before filling his head.
A wise man fills his head before emptying his heart.
The leopard was too quick to show his true heart.
The heart of a wise man lies quiet like limpid water

Mom: Who knows why we use chickens for sacrifice?
Ngeh: We don't know. Tell us.
Akamin: Tell us so that we may also know.
Mom: Give me a chief.
Akamin: I give you Chief Memba of Asalakung
Mom: I refuse. He is a sheep. He has done a lot of foolish things.
He is not the kind of shepherd who prevents attacks from foxes.
Dad: Doesn't he have counsellors? Doesn't Asalakung have a council?
Other people's wisdom prevents the king from being called a fool.
Mom: Whether or not, I still refuse him, that Chief Memba of Asal-
akung.
When a village chief himself goes around inviting people to a meeting
Know that there is something wrong with the system that must be
fixed.
Give me another chief, a good one, or my story will remain in my
stomach.
Ngeh: I give you Chief Ngalagu, the brave lion of Achimbong.
Mom: I accept. He is not the kind of man who stays home with his
wives
When poisoned spears are flying in different directions in blazing
fields
After the drums of war have been beaten calling men to take up arms.
So here comes the story that says why people use chickens for sacrific-
es.

Akamin: Yes, we are ready for it. Tell us so that we may also know.
Mom: Yes, open your ears for it. I also heard it from my own mother.
Once upon a time, many things were going wrong in the world of men
People did not exactly know why these things were going wrong,
Why there were so many bad and evil things happening in their land.
So, they called a meeting on a certain day to decide on what to do.
At the meeting it was revealed that their ancestors were not happy with them
So, they had to offer sacrifices to appease their ancestors and avert further evil.
It was revealed that the sacrifices required the use of an animal as a bait.
So, what animal were they to use? The question was on everyone's mind.
They then appealed to animals to offer one of theirs to be used for sacrifices.
The animals took pity on men and called a meeting to come to their rescue.
On the day of the meeting all the animals were present except the chicken.
It said it was too busy to attend and that it will agree with any decision
That the rest of the animals would take to solve the problems men were facing.
Given that the chicken was absent from the meeting, it was the chosen one.
All the animals agreed that henceforth men will use chickens for their sacrifices.
That is why people use chickens for sacrifices in bad as well as good moments.
Dad: Those who are absent are always wrong in the eyes of those who are present.

Akamin: Dad, why did Ndem, the creator of the universe and all things in it,
Not create chickens and those who sit in meetings nodding their heads like lizards

The way he created the chameleon who looks in all directions before
moving?
Is it even known that just because the lizard nods his head, as he often
does
Does not mean that he is in agreement with what goes on around
him?
Why did Ndem not create chickens and those who parrot lyrics from
above
The way he created the praying mantis who looks in all directions
before it leaps?

Dad: All heads were created the same, but not all thoughts are the
same.
Trees of various kinds and sizes are in our dense forest for all to climb.
Some climb to the top of trees from where they can talk with the sun
The earth will wait for those who insist on going beyond the top of
trees.

Akamin: But, dad, I thought you had a tale for us.
The moon will soon go to sleep and I hear owls hooting on trees far
away.
Dad: Yes, the story of the battle of Kongofata, the land of seven hills
and valleys.
A long time ago, the Agovi and the Bushi were great enemies.
They used to raid each other in order to obtain more farmland and
cattle.
One day the Agovi organised a raid on the Bushi to once more show
their might.
All men were supposed to take part in the battle, except the old and
the handicapped.
On that particular day, the leader gave the final instructions to the
raiding party
And the oldest man in the land of the Agovi gave his blessings to the
warriors.
As they marched off, they sang war songs and uttered electrifying war
cries
Wielding their spears and clubs like a guild of hunters on an elephant

hunt
Boasting how they will mow down their enemies within minutes into the battle.
Some claimed that the Bushi warriors were cowards
And would tremble at the sight of the powerful Agovi warriors.
They recalled the many times they had defeated them
And this time they knew for sure that victory would be theirs.
However, the day was not a good one for them.
The weather looked dull; nimbus covered the face of the earth.
A dark cloud kept hovering in the horizon and the sun went behind it.
A child of one of the Agovis developed an epileptic fit, all of a sudden,
And the father decided to stay home because it was a bad omen.
Another man went back home when a chameleon crossed their path.
Some warriors returned when they saw owls following them.
Many did not however yield to the temptation of calling off the battle.
They regarded those who went back as cowards and traitors.
The Bushi, at the same time, were busy organising themselves.
Their spies had announced the coming of the enemies.
They quickly moved their herds, flocks, women and children to safety.
In order to reach the Bushi territory, the Agovi had to pass through
A narrow path enclosed by huge rocks and hills on both sides.
There was no other entrance into Bushi territory apart from this one.
The Agovi warriors confidently marched in and advanced towards Bushi.
They were surprised by the quietness of the area
They concluded that the cowardly Bushis had taken to their heels.
But the Bushi warriors had been waiting for all of them to enter
So as to block the entrance and bar them from retreating.
Other warriors were to attack as soon as the signal was given.
The Agovi were taken by surprise and slain in large numbers.
This was the saddest period the Agovi people have ever known.
They have never forgotten this day in their history.
This is the end of the story.

The household kept quiet, lost in the legend.
Fireflies fought the night with their splendid light
Crickets were busy chirping away in nearby bushes

And the moon began to fade away in the misty sky
Leaving the world to darkness and to me.

The Day You Shall Finally Leave

The day you shall finally leave
Your cherished Hallelujah Choir
Pitch-dark in a shed as grey as ash,
Lost in your legend as trite as blunt blades,
Will negotiate a pitch bend, hertz after hertz,
That appeals only to sextons as pale as death.

That lucky day you shall finally leave
Mice will leave holes and purr like cats,
Pigs will leave sties and howl like wolves,
Wrens will leave nests and scream like eagles,
Sheep will leave pens and chatter like monkeys,
And walls will cease to have the ears of elephants.

Yes, that lucky day you shall leave for good
Dogs won't sniff at innocent mortals any more,
They will sniff where there is nice food for them.
That lucky day you shall finally leave for good
Cockroaches won't fear the fierce sun any more,
They will spring like cats to play against cocks.

Yes, that lucky day you shall leave us for good
Playgrounds, vast as the sea, shall be even for all,
Not spiky like the chameleon's back, hard to tread on.
That lucky day you shall finally leave, yes that day,
The spider's web shall be used to rest dry old bones
As well as a food trap for weary toothless rodents.

The Resurrection

On a certain Monday, when the day was red hot
Re bathed some animals on earth with the White Nile
And gave them white ants to eat, and they turned cream
Like a pale plate floating in a grey midnight sky.

Aton showed up the next day in the heart of darkness
And bathed the remaining ones with the Blue Nile
And gave them black ants to eat, and they turned dark
Like the hard case of dung beetle glittering on an anthill.

Then **Osiris** emerged on Wednesday as the animals sat down to eat
Raining down a lecture as to why animals shouldn't live on ants alone
As though being in the forest they see only one tree to lean on, arguing that
When a lion can't find flesh to feed on, it has no choice but to eat grass.

So from Thursday **Osiris** kept giving them worms for breakfast,
Frogs for lunch and toads for supper – till kingdom come –
As though all apes in the woods know only fruits and nothing else;
As though they are like penguins who love only seafood and nothing else.

Tired of the constant menu, bent on sending **Osiris** packing home,
The animals let loose their poisoned spears on his body, on Friday,
A day monkeys die when all trees in the forest are slippery,
A day a brave leopard dies when betrayed by a sly old fox.

The animals gathered the next day at a time when mushrooms sprout from the earth
Those of the air, those on land, those in water; the males, the females; the young, the old;

To decide what menu suits each of their kind, to decide what food goes with who.
And they all agreed to walk in the path of their forefathers, to eat and drink like them.

Osiris emerged from his tomb on Sunday, like a confident mole from its hole,
And returned to his home beneath the hills and forests where he was lord and king,
And then it dawned on all the animals – the clever, the foolish; the wise, the stupid –
That you don't punish a fish by throwing it in water.

You Too May Carry A Cross

Dazzling
Mansions
Rainbow
Castles on
Grim earth
Posh hotels
For you alone while kwashiorkor children
Comb grey fields for free mushrooms and
Juicy termites for their mothers' soup pots.
Does it mean
Much to you
When many
Sleep under
Cotton tress
In open air,
Straw huts,
On mats or
Cane beds?
Now that it
Has never
Bothered you
For once Sir
You will surely
Carry a cross.

The tongue
Was made
For tasting
Swallowing
And speaking.
But Sir, Sir,
You stick yours out at people like that of the
Green mamba about to strike a faultless prey
Or that of a mad dragon spitting roaring fire.
Does it occur
To you Sir that
Strong people
Stand not for
Themselves
But for others?
Do you know
That the fall of
A dry leaf is a
Warning to the
Green ones?
If you do not
Truly know Sir
You will surely
Carry a cross.

Like a lone
High-rise
Overlooking
The Atlantic
You carry
Shoulders
Around, bluffing like a eunuch before a lass
With nothing to show except his lord's lush
Castle under his watch, inherited years ago.
Does it occur
To you Sir that
A razor may
Be sharper than
An axe but it
Cannot cut wood?
Sir, does it occur
To you that no
Matter how tall
A man may be
He cannot see
Tomorrow?
If it hasn't Sir
You will surely
Carry a cross.

         Is anything
        In a skirt fine
        Meat to eat?
        Do lions eat
       Grass if they
        Do not find
Meat Sir? Do not let eyelashes capture you.
The feathers of peacocks conceal their pride
Just as eyelashes may conceal conjunctivitis.
       Sir, does it occur
       To you that the
       Surface of water
       Is beautiful but
        It is not good
         To sleep on?
        Do you know
        That the skin
       Of a leopard is
        Beautiful but
        Not his heart?
       If you don't Sir
      Know today that
       You will surely
        Carry a cross.

You feel hurt
When called
Names of all
Sorts thought
To define who
You really are:
Black scorpion, sly fox, slippery eel, mad
Hornet, thirsty bug, stubborn mule, curious
Lynx, hungry bear, crazy loom, shrewd kite.
Sir, does it occur
To you that you
Foam like an
Angry river and
Surge like a hot
Tempest instead
Of staying mute
Like an iceberg?
You bear grudges
As if politics is a
Dog eat dog feat.
Know today that
If change comes
You will surely
Carry a cross.

What do Amos,
Isaiah & Luke
Tell you about
Intoxicants Sir?
What do Job &
Jeremiah teach
You about the excessive intake of strong gin
And other intoxicants that make people walk
Like stray dogs in a noisy rush-hour traffic?
Sir, does it occur
To you that drunks
Take any dog for a
Bitch to prey on?
Is *in vino veritas* a
Saying that justifies
Rising up early in
A cold morning to
Chase hot drinks?
Do bears seek the
Sahara in winter?
If you don't know
The right answers
You will surely
Carry a cross.

About the Author

Nol Alembong is Professor of African Literature and Cultural Studies and current Vice-Chancellor of Fomic Polytechnic University with campuses in Buea and Douala, Cameroon. He is the author of three other volumes of poetry, *The Passing Wind* (1991; revised 2014), *Forest Echoes* (2010) and *Green Call* (2017).

About the Publisher

Spears Books is an independent publisher dedicated to providing innovative publication strategies with emphasis on Africana stories and perspectives. As a platform for alternative voices, we prioritize the accessibility and affordability of our titles to ensure that relevant and often marginal voices are represented at the global marketplace of ideas. Our titles – poetry, fiction, narrative nonfiction, memoirs, reference, travel writing, African languages, and young people's literature – aim to bring African worldviews closer to diverse readers. Our titles are distributed in paperback and electronic formats globally by African Books Collective.

Connect with Us: Go to www.spearsbooks.org to learn about exclusive previews and read excerpts of new books, find detailed information on our titles, authors, subject area books, and special discounts.

Subscribe to our Free Newsletter: Be amongst the first to hear about our newest publications, special discount offers, news about bestsellers, author interviews, coupons and more! Subscribe to our newsletter by visiting www.spearsbooks.org

Quantity Discounts: Spears Books are available at quantity discounts for orders of ten or more copies. Contact Spears Books at orders@spears-media.com.

Host a Reading Group: Learn more about how to host a reading group on our website at www.spearsbooks.org

www.ingramcontent.com/pod-product-compliance
Lightning Source LLC
Chambersburg PA
CBHW022144160426
43197CB00009B/1419